THE POWER OF FORGIVENESS

by Edith Bajema

Grand Rapids, Michigan

Unless otherwise indicated, Scripture quotations in this publication are from the HOLY BIBLE, NEW INTERNATIONAL VERSION, © 1973, 1978, 1984, International Bible Society. Used by permission of Zondervan Bible Publishers.

Cover photo by PhotoDisc.

Faith Alive Christian Resources published by CRC Publications.
Discover Your Bible series. *Discover the Power of Forgiveness,* © 2001 by CRC Publications, 2850 Kalamazoo Ave. SE, Grand Rapids, MI 49560. All rights reserved. With the exception of brief excerpts for review purposes, no part of this book may be reproduced in any manner whatsoever without written permission from the publisher. Printed in the United States of America on recycled paper. ⊕

We welcome your comments. Call us at 1-800-333-8300 or e-mail us at editors@faithaliveresources.org.

ISBN 1-56212-803-5

10 9 8 7 6 5 4 3 2

Contents

How to Study 4

Introduction 5

Glossary of Terms 7

Lesson 1
The Power of God's Forgiveness 8

Lesson 2
The Response of the Forgiven Heart 11

Lesson 3
How Many Times? 14

Lesson 4
The Hidden Power of Forgiveness 18

Lesson 5
Stories of Forgiveness 21

Lesson 6
The Good News: Receiving and Giving Forgiveness 26

Evaluation Questionnaire

How to Study

The questions in this study booklet will help you discover for yourself what the Bible says. This is inductive Bible study—no one will tell you what the Bible says or what to believe. You will discover the message for yourself.

Questions are the key to inductive Bible study. Through questions you will search for the writers' thoughts and ideas. The prepared questions in this booklet are designed to help you in your quest for answers. You can and should ask your own questions too. The Bible comes alive with meaning for many people as they discover for themselves the exciting truths it contains. Our hope and prayer is that this booklet will help the Bible come alive for you.

The questions in this study are designed to be used with the New International Version of the Bible, but other translations can also be used.

Step 1. Read the Bible passage several times. Allow the thoughts and ideas to sink in. Think about its meaning. Ask questions of your own about the passage.

Step 2. Answer the questions, drawing your answers from the passage. Remember that the purpose of the study is to discover what the Bible says. Write your answers in your own words. If you use Bible study aids such as commentaries or Bible handbooks, do so only after completing your own personal study.

Step 3. Apply the Bible's message to your own life and world. Ask yourself these questions: What is this passage saying to me? How does it challenge me? Comfort me? Encourage me? Is there a promise I should claim? A warning I should heed? For what can I give thanks? If you sense God speaking to you in some way, respond to God in a personal prayer.

Step 4. Share your thoughts with someone else if possible. This will be easiest if you are part of a Bible study group that meets regularly to share discoveries and discuss questions. If you would like to learn of a study group in your area or if you would like more information on how to start a small group Bible study, write to Discover Your Bible, 2850 Kalamazoo Ave. SE, Grand Rapids, MI 49560 or to P.O. Box 5070, STN LCD 1, Burlington, ON L7R 3Y8, or visit www.FaithAliveResources.org.

Introduction

Someone has done you wrong—perhaps a deep wrong. You have been hurt more than you care to admit, even to close friends. The memory of that hurt feels like a bruise on your spirit, a crushed area that remains tender and bleeding, even though weeks, months, or even years have passed.

You try not to think about it too much, because it makes you feel sad or angry. You may forget about it for days on end. Life may seem to go on as it did before—until you see that person again. Suddenly all the hurt and anger come to the surface, and the memory of your hurt is as fresh and painful as on the day it happened.

Against that person, your heart remains angry and bitter and confused. How could your friend or coworker or family member or neighbor have wronged you like that? What can you do to show that person how his or her actions made you feel? How can you teach a lesson in return? How can you pay back a little of what you received?

So a root of bitterness springs up. It may be just a little root, or it may be large—but it finds a place to grow in the soil of your heart.

Sometimes this root of bitterness, this unforgiving spirit, will grow until it kills a relationship that once was loving. Sometimes it grows large enough to kill the spirit of the person who harbors it. It becomes a prison, and those caught in it are unable to free themselves.

There is a key that will open the prison and free your spirit. It is the key of forgiveness. It will let you out of the small, dark place that your spirit has been trapped, and bring you out into the light, into the open spaces of God's love. You will find healing—and will find that others are unexpectedly blessed by the change in your heart.

Come and sit by God's side for a while, and look into the deep places of his forgiving heart. Listen to Jesus talk to his friends about forgiveness. Eavesdrop on how members of the early Christian church were taught to get along with each other in spite of their differences.

Then open your heart to discover the healing power of forgiveness in your own life.

—Edith Bajema
Grand Rapids, Michigan

Recommended Resource

It will be clear by the end of this study, if it is not already clear, that a six-lesson study on forgiveness can only begin to answer some of the tough questions on forgiveness. One excellent resource is Lewis Smedes's *The Art of Forgiving* (New York: Ballantine Books, 1996). You may find it helpful to read Smedes's book side by side with this study, as it expands on many questions that your group members will certainly have.

Glossary of Terms

denarii—Jewish coins in use during Roman times. A hundred denarii would equal a few dollars in today's North American economy.

grace—undeserved favor, kindness, and love.

holy—set apart from others by being pure, free from iniquity, cleansed, and ready to do God's will.

hyssop—a plant that grew in Egypt, in the Sinai Desert, and in Palestine that was capable of producing a stem three or four feet in length.

iniquity—sin; disobedience to God's will.

kingdom of heaven—God's active rule over the creation that becomes visible wherever places, people, and relationships are devoted to obeying the Lord Jesus Christ. Can refer both to the angels and spirits in heaven and to people on earth who seek to live the way God intended.

mercy—compassion and kindness that is not deserved; often used as reference to forgiving a debt.

Pharisee—a member of the Jewish religious sect that emphasized the importance of keeping even the smallest of religious laws and rituals. Some Pharisees were known for their legalism and hypocrisy.

prophet—one who speaks for God or comes with a message from God.

righteous—free from guilt or sin. God regards people who are joined to God by faith as righteous through Christ.

sin—an action or thought that misses the mark of God's perfect standard for our lives. Sin results in a broken relationship with God.

sinner—one who sins.

talent—a measure of gold, much larger than a denarius; a thousand talents would equal millions of dollars in North American currency.

tax collectors—Jews who agreed to serve the hated Roman government by collecting tax from their fellow Jews; they were expected to keep a portion of the taxes for their own pockets.

transgression—see **sin**.

uncircumcision—the state of not being circumcised. Circumcision was the physical sign of belonging to God's covenant people; it implied purity and being set apart from the rest of the world.

Lesson 1
Psalm 103:1-5, 7-12; Proverbs 20:9; 1 John 1:9; Psalm 130:3-4; Colossians 2:13-14

The Power of God's Forgiveness

1. *Psalm 103:1-5*

   a. What is the psalm writer encouraging himself to do?

   b. What benefits has he received from God?

2. *Psalm 103:7-10*

   a. How does God show compassion?

   b. How does God respond to people when they sin?

3. *Psalm 103:11-12*
   a. How great is God's love toward those who fear God?

   b. What happens to the transgressions of those who have this kind of relationship with God?

4. *Proverbs 20:9*
   a. What does this question imply about all people?

   b. Do you believe there is anyone who can truthfully say this? Why or why not?

5. *1 John 1:9*
   a. How does this verse echo Proverbs 20:9?

   b. What comfort is there in this verse?

6. **Psalm 130:3-4**
    a. What does verse 3 imply about all people? About God?

    b. What quality of God allows people to have a relationship with God?

7. **Colossians 2:13-14**
    a. How does this verse describe the condition of people before they were forgiven by God?

    b. What did God do for these people? How?

8. **Psalm 103:1-5, 7-12; Proverbs 20:9; 1 John 1:9; Psalm 130:3-4; Colossians 2:13-14**
    a. What do these passages tell us about the human condition? About God?

    b. What is the key to a restored relationship with God?

Lesson 2
Luke 7:36-50; Psalm 32:1-7

The Response of the Forgiven Heart

1. *Luke 7:36-39*

   The Pharisees were a religious sect in Jewish society. They studied the religious laws and regulations thoroughly and tried to obey them perfectly. They were also known for their emphasis on public appearance and for their tendency to condemn those who did not keep the law as strictly as they did.

   a. Who invites Jesus to dinner?

   b. Who enters as an uninvited guest? What does she do?

   c. What is the Pharisee's response? What does this suggest about him?

2. *Luke 7:40-43*

   a. What story does Jesus tell?

   b. What does the story tell us about forgiveness?

3. *Luke 7:44-50*
   a. How does Jesus apply the story to Simon? To the woman?

   b. What does this story tell us about the response of the forgiven heart?

4. *Psalm 32:1-2*
   a. What kind of person is blessed, according to these verses?

   b. How does the writer describe the meaning of forgiveness?

   c. Why do you think the writer mentions deceit (v. 2) along with transgression and sin?

5. *Psalm 32:3-5*
   a. What had the writer kept silent about?

b. How does he describe his condition during this time?

c. What changed this?

6. *Psalm 32:6-7*
   a. What changes in a person's relationship to God when they confess their wrongdoing? Why do you think this is?

   b. What does God become for such people?

7. *Luke 7:36-50; Psalm 32:1-7*
   a. What do these passages teach about God?

   b. What do they reveal about those who have received God's forgiveness?

Lesson 3

Matthew 18:21-35; Ephesians 4:32; 1 Corinthians 13:4-7

How Many Times?

1. *Matthew 18:21-22*

    a. What question does Peter ask Jesus?

    b. What appears to be his attitude toward forgiveness?

    c. What is Jesus' answer?

    d. What do you think this means?

2. *Matthew 18:23-27*

    A sum of ten thousand talents equals millions of dollars in North American currency today. Given the economic status of servants in that society, this sum would have taken several lifetimes to accumulate.

    a. Why might Jesus feel a story is needed here?

b. To what does he compare the kingdom of heaven?

c. How much does the servant owe his master? What could happen to him?

d. What happens to this debt? Why?

3. *Matthew 18:28-31*

   A hundred denarii would equal a few dollars in today's North American economy.

   a. What is the servant's first action after his debt has been forgiven?

   b. What does this tell us about him?

   c. How do his actions make others feel? How would you have felt?

4. *Matthew 18:32-35*
   a. What does the king do when he hears the news? Why?

   b. How does Jesus compare this story to the kingdom of heaven?

5. *Ephesians 4:32*
   a. What is to be the attitude of Christians toward each other?

   b. What is to be the basis for their forgiveness?

6. *1 Corinthians 13:4-7*
   a. How do these verses describe God?

   b. What does love have to do with forgiveness?

   c. What do you find challenging about this passage?

7. *Matthew 18:21-35; Ephesians 4:32; 1 Corinthians 13:4-7*
   a. What have you learned about forgiveness in this lesson?

   b. What have you learned about God? About yourself?

Lesson 4
Matthew 18:15-17; 5:43-48; Romans 12:17-21; Hebrews 12:14-15; 1 Peter 3:8-9

The Hidden Power of Forgiveness

1. *Matthew 18:15-17*
   a. What does Jesus tell his followers to do when another believer sins against them?

   b. What happens when the offender does not want to be reconciled?

   c. Do you think this is a good process? Why or why not?

2. *Matthew 5:43-48*
   a. How do people normally treat their enemies, according to this verse?

   b. How does Jesus want his followers to treat their enemies?

c. What reasoning does he give for this?

3. *Romans 12:17-21*
   a. How are Christians to respond to those who do evil to them?

   b. What is God's role, according to these verses?

   c. What is the ultimate outcome?

4. *Hebrews 12:14-15*
   a. What should others see in the believer's life and behavior?

   b. What happens when a Christian misses the grace of God?

5. **1 Peter 3:8-9**
   a. What qualities are to mark Christian relationships?

   b. What reward is promised?

6. **Matthew 18:15-17; 5:43-48; Romans 12:17-21; Hebrews 12:14-15; 1 Peter 3:8-9**
   a. What things did you learn from these Scripture passages?

   b. What did you struggle with the most?

   c. How might these passages apply to people in your life?

Lesson 5

Genesis 37:2-8, 17b-28; 41:46-49, 53-57; 42:1-7a; 45:1-5; 50:15-20; Luke 23:32-34

Stories of Forgiveness

1. *Genesis 37:2-8*

   a. What things have created a bad relationship between Joseph and his brothers?

   b. How do these illustrate underlying problems that can destroy relationships?

2. *Genesis 37:17b-28*

   a. What plan do the brothers make when they see Joseph coming?

   b. What does this tell us about their feelings toward Joseph?

   c. How do their plans change?

d. How would you characterize Joseph's brothers, based on these verses?

3. *Genesis 41:46-49, 53-57; 42:1-7a*

After his brothers sell Joseph to the Ishmaelites, the Ishmaelites in turn sell Joseph to an Egyptian official named Potiphar. Potiphar likes Joseph and elevates him to a place of high responsibility, until Potiphar's wife unfairly accuses Joseph of trying to sleep with her. Joseph is put in prison, where he proves himself trustworthy to the prison wardens and becomes known for his God-given ability to interpret dreams.

After about ten years, God gives Pharaoh, the ruler of Egypt, a dream about seven fat cows and seven lean cows, and Joseph is asked to interpret the meaning. Joseph is able, with God's help, to warn Pharaoh of seven years of severe famine that will follow seven years of great plenty. Pharaoh is so impressed with Joseph that he makes him the highest official in the land, second in power only to Pharaoh himself.

a. What crucial role does Joseph play in Egypt's history?

b. How does Joseph's importance extend beyond Egypt?

c. How is Joseph's dream fulfilled?

4. *Genesis 45:1-5*

   Joseph recognizes his brothers, but they do not recognize him. So Joseph decides to test their hearts before revealing his identity to them. He lays an elaborate scheme to get them to bring Benjamin, his little brother and now his father's favorite, to Egypt. Then he tests them to see if they will betray and desert Benjamin as they had Joseph years earlier.

   His plan shows that his brothers have indeed changed. One of them even offers his own life in the place of Benjamin's, and pleads with the Egyptian ruler to let Benjamin return to his father. Joseph is overcome with emotion, and can no longer keep his identity secret.

   a. What are Joseph's feelings when he finally reveals himself to his brothers?

   b. What attitude does Joseph show toward them?

   c. What role has God played in these events, according to Joseph?

5. *Genesis 50:15-20*

   Joseph brings his father, his brothers, and all their families to live in the land of Egypt, in the province of Goshen. There they have enough food and good land for their herds and flocks. Jacob, Joseph's father, lives for seventeen more years in Egypt before he dies.

   a. What do Joseph's brothers fear after their father's death?

b. What does Joseph do when he receives their message? How does he answer them?

c. What does he see as God's role in all this?

d. What have you learned about Joseph's character in this story?

6. *Luke 23:32-34*

   Jesus, the Son of God, became human and was born as a baby to an Israelite woman, Mary. At age thirty he began his ministry of working miracles and teaching people about the kingdom of God. After three years Jesus was brought to trial by his own people. He was condemned on false charges and sentenced to death on a cross—a criminal's death. Jesus submitted to this, knowing that his innocent and willing death would pay the penalty for the sins of all people who receive God's offer of forgiveness.

   a. What is happening to Jesus?

   b. What is his concern for those who are crucifying him?

c. What example does Jesus set for his followers?

7. *Genesis 37:2-8, 17b-28; 41:46-49, 53-57; 42:1-7a; 45:1-5; 50:15-20; Luke 23:32-34*

   a. What have you learned about forgiveness from these stories?

   b. Do you have any stories from your own life or from the life of someone you know that may teach something about forgiveness?

Lesson 6
Psalm 51:1-17; Mark 11:25

The Good News: Receiving and Giving Forgiveness

1. *Psalm 51:1-2*
   a. What is the spirit, or feeling, of this passage?

   b. What does this prayer ask God to do?

   c. What qualities of God are mentioned in these verses?

   d. What does this prayer tell you about the one who is praying it?

2. *Psalm 51:3-6*
   a. What is troubling the writer of this psalm?

b. What does he acknowledge about God in these verses? About himself?

c. At what level did God want to work in his life?

3. **Psalm 51:7-9**

    Hyssop is a member of the mint family; it has a fresh, clean fragrance and small white flowers. The leaves and stem are covered with tiny hairs, which hold droplets when the plant is dipped into liquid. The Israelites used the hyssop plant to sprinkle blood or water during times of spiritual purification and cleansing (see Ex. 12:22; Lev. 14; Num. 19).

    a. What changes does the writer of this psalm ask God to make?

    b. What pictures does he use to describe God's forgiveness?

4. **Psalm 51:10-12**

    a. What hope does verse 10 offer?

b. What is the writer's concern regarding his relationship to God?

5. **Psalm 51:13-17**

   a. What happens to someone who has been forgiven by God?

   b. What does God really value?

6. **Mark 11:25**

   a. What must we be aware of when we pray to our Father, according to Jesus?

   b. What happens when we offer forgiveness to someone who has offended or hurt us?

   c. How does this verse relate to Jesus' story of the unforgiving servant?

7. *Psalm 51:1-17; Mark 11:25*

   a. How is God's forgiveness related to our forgiveness of others?

   b. What have you learned about forgiveness that relates to your own life? Are there areas in which you need God's forgiveness? Are there people in your life you would like to be able to forgive?

Wrap-Up

The following words may be helpful as you consider this study:

Listen now to what God is saying to you.

You may be aware of things in your life that keep you from coming near to God. You may have thought of God as someone who is unsympathetic and unforgiving. You may feel like you don't know how to pray to God or how to come near to God.

Look at what God has shown you in this lesson. You are precious. Jesus died to redeem you from your sin. Jesus bought you at a price. Jesus wants you to belong to him and be a part of his family. God the Father has been watching over you and caring for you; God desires to forgive you. God loves you so much that he gave his only Son, so that by believing in Jesus you can accept his gift of eternal life. The Holy Spirit has been at work in your heart, drawing you closer to God. The Spirit wants to help you with this decision and give you a new life of freedom and joy in Christ.

So now accept God's forgiveness and come near to God. It's as simple as A-B-C:

- **A**dmit that you have sinned, and that you need God's forgiveness.
- **B**elieve that God loves you and that Jesus already paid the price for your sins.
- **C**ommit your life to God in prayer, asking God to forgive your sins, to make you his child, and to fill you with the Holy Spirit."

Prayer of Commitment

Here is a prayer of commitment to Jesus Christ as Savior. If you long to be in a loving relationship with Jesus Christ, pray this prayer. If you have already made that commitment to Jesus, use it for renewal and praise.

Dear God, I come to you simply and honestly to confess that I have sinned, that sin is a part of who I am. And yet I know that you listen to sinners who are truthful before you. And so I come with empty hands and heart, asking for forgiveness.

I confess that only through faith in Jesus Christ can I come to you. I confess my need for a Savior, and I thank you, Jesus Christ, for dying on the cross to pay the price for my sins. I ask that you forgive my sins, and count me among those who are righteous in your sight. Remove the guilt that accompanies sin and bring me to our heavenly Father.

Give me your Holy Spirit now, to help me pray and to teach me from your Word. Be my faithful God and help me to serve you faithfully. In the name of Jesus Christ, I pray. Amen.

Evaluation Questionnaire

DISCOVER THE POWER OF FORGIVENESS

As you complete this study, please fill out this questionnaire to help us evaluate the effectiveness of our materials. Please be candid. Thank you.

1. Was this a home group ___ or a church-based ___ program? What church?

2. Was the study used for
   ___ a community evangelism group?
   ___ a community grow group?
   ___ a church Bible study group?

3. How would you rate the materials?

   Study Guide
   ___ excellent ___ very good ___ good ___ fair ___ poor

   Leader Guide
   ___ excellent ___ very good ___ good ___ fair ___ poor

4. What were the strengths?

5. What were the weaknesses?

6. What would you suggest to improve the material?

7. In general, what was the experience of your group?

Your name (optional)_____

Address _____

_____

8. Other comments:

(Please fold, tape, stamp, and mail. Thank you.)

Faith Alive Christian Resources
2850 Kalamazoo Ave. SE
Grand Rapids, MI 49560